Scary Creatures
SPIDERS,
INSECTS, and MINIBEASTS

Written by
Penny Clarke

Illustrated by
Mark Bergin

W
FRANKLIN WATTS
A Division of Scholastic Inc.
NEW YORK • TORONTO • LONDON • AUCKLAND • SYDNEY
MEXICO CITY • NEW DELHI • HONG KONG
DANBURY, CONNECTICUT

Created and designed by
David Salariya

Author:

Penny Clarke is an author and editor specializing in nonfiction books for children. The books she has written include titles on natural history, rainforests, and volcanoes, as well as others on different periods of history. She use to live in central London, but thanks to modern technology she has now realized her dream of being able to live and work in the countryside.

Artist:

Mark Bergin was born in Hastings, England, in 1961. He studied at Eastbourne College of Art and has illustrated many children's nonfiction books. He lives in Bexhill-on-Sea, England, with his wife and three children.

Additional Artists:

David Antram
Lizzie Harper
Pam Hewetson
Sean Milne
Carolyn Scrace
David Stewart

Series creator:

David Salariya was born in Dundee, Scotland. In 1989, he established The Salariya Book Company. He has illustrated a wide range of books and has created many new series for publishers in the U.K. and overseas. He lives in Brighton, England, with his wife, illustrator Shirley Willis, and their son.

Consultant:

Dr. Gerald Legg holds a doctorate in zoology from Manchester University. He worked in West Africa for several years as a lecturer and rainforest researcher. His current position is biologist at the Booth Museum of Natural History in Brighton. He is also the author of many natural history books for children.

Editor: Karen Barker Smith

Picture Research: Nicky Roe

Photo Credits:

A.N.T, NHPA: 7
Anthony Bannister, NHPA: 15
Daniel Heuclin, NHPA: 17, 27
Image Quest 3-D, NHPA: 21
Hellio & Van Ingen, NHPA: 19
Yves Lanceau, NHPA: 5
PhotoDisc: 22
PhotoSpin.com: 26

Created, designed, and produced by
The Salariya Book Company Ltd
Book House,
25 Marlborough Place
Brighton BN1 1UB

Visit the Salariya Book Company at
www.salariya.com

A CIP catalog record for this title is available from the Library of Congress.

ISBN 0-531-14674-X (Lib. Bdg.)
ISBN 0-531-14850-5 (Pbk.)

Published in the United States by Franklin Watts
A Division of Scholastic Inc.
90 Sherman Turnpike
Danbury, CT 06816

Printed in China.

Printed on paper from sustainable forests.

Contents

What Are Spiders, Insects, and Minibeasts?

"Minibeast" is a word used for any small creepy-crawly. That means there are a lot of minibeasts around – there are over a million **species** of insect and 40,000 species of spider – and those are just the ones we know about. If both spiders and insects are minibeasts, how can you tell the difference between the two? Spiders always have eight legs and insects always have six.

Are beetles insects?

Beetles are insects because they have six legs. All beetles have the same four-stage life cycle. The eggs hatch into wormlike **larvae**, or grubs. After awhile each larva turns into a **pupa** from which the adult emerges.

Yes, beetles are insects.

Male stag beetles (right) get their name from the males' antlerlike **mandibles**, or jaws. They fight other males with these "antlers," just as stags do.

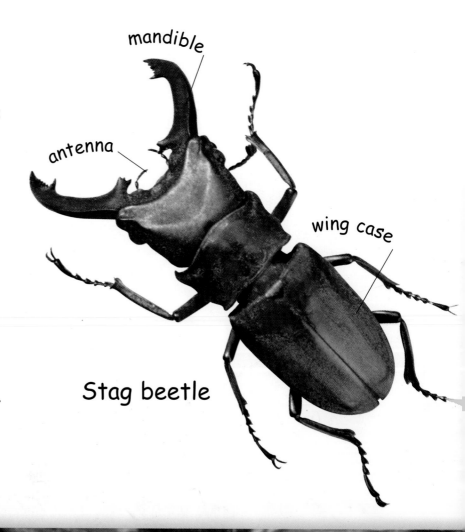

mandible

antenna

wing case

Stag beetle

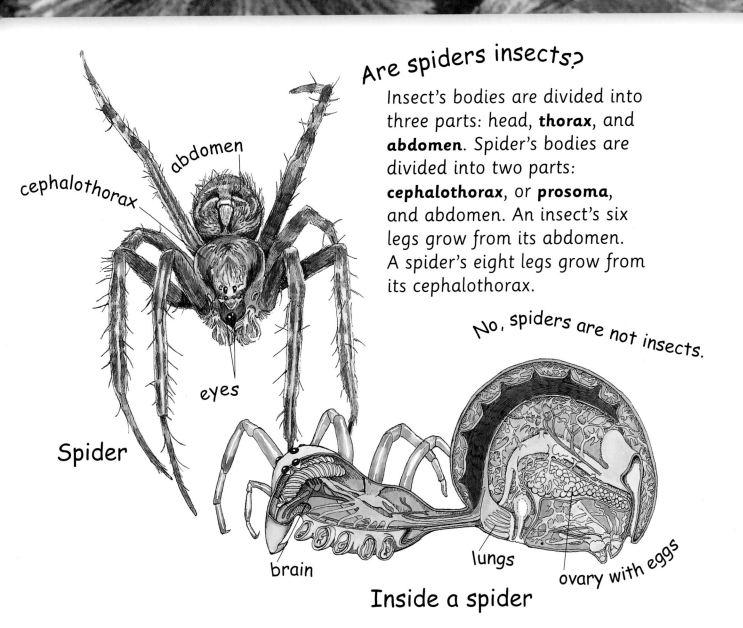

Are spiders insects?

Insect's bodies are divided into three parts: head, **thorax**, and **abdomen**. Spider's bodies are divided into two parts: **cephalothorax**, or **prosoma**, and abdomen. An insect's six legs grow from its abdomen. A spider's eight legs grow from its cephalothorax.

No, spiders are not insects.

abdomen

cephalothorax

eyes

Spider

brain

lungs

ovary with eggs

Inside a spider

Did You Know?

There are 20,000 species of wasp worldwide. Hornets are the largest, measuring up to 2 inches (4 cm) long. The three different parts of the hornet's body can clearly be seen (right). This means that hornets are insects.

head   thorax   abdomen

Hornet feeding on a peach

Why Are Spiders Scary?

Millions of people around the world suffer from **arachnophobia**, which means "fear of spiders." But why? Spiders are not big. The largest is smaller than a person's hand. Perhaps they are scary because they are silent, seem to appear from nowhere, and some are poisonous to humans.

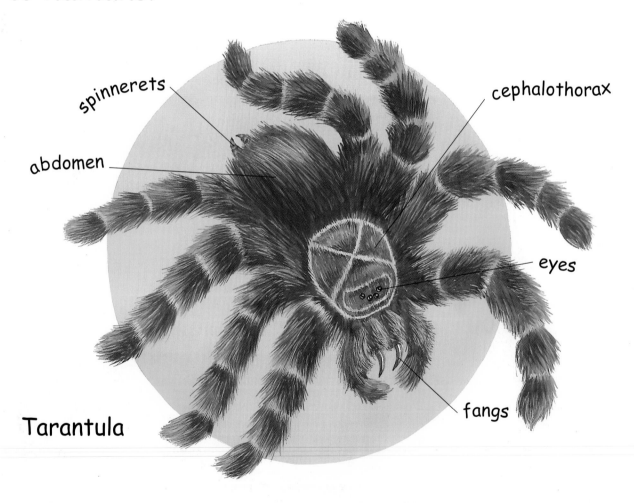

spinnerets

abdomen

cephalothorax

eyes

fangs

Tarantula

Tarantulas are the largest type of spider. Some species measure over 5 inches (13 cm) long including their legs. They pounce on their prey and inject it with poison.

Centuries ago people believed that if a spider bit a human, the only way to get rid of the poison was to sweat it out of the body by dancing the tarantella, which is a very fast dance.

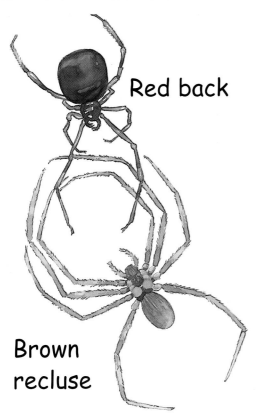

Red back

Brown recluse

Very poisonous spiders, such as the red back and brown recluse (left), like living in the nooks and crannies of people's homes. That makes them very scary because you never know where you'll find them.

Did You Know?

The bite of the Australian black funnel web spider (below) can kill a human. It spins its funnel-shaped web on the ground and waits for its insect **prey** at one end. There are spiders that make funnel webs in other parts of the world, but they are only poisonous to their prey.

Black funnel web spider

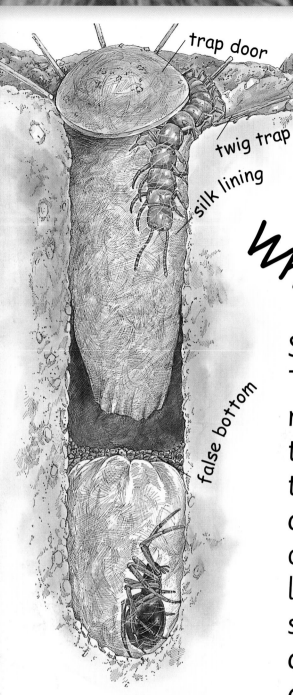

trap door

twig trap

silk lining

false bottom

Trap-door spider
in its hole

X-Ray Vision

Hold the next page up to the light and see what's inside the spider's web.

See what's inside

Where Do Spiders Live?

Spiders live all over the world. They are **cold-blooded**, which means they need the temperature of the air around them to keep them warm. They cannot live in very cold places or on very high mountains. Spiders live in a wide range of **habitats** such as houses, tropical forests, caves, deserts, woodlands, grassy plains, in the ground, and even in ponds and rivers. Spiders do not live in the sea.

The trap-door spider (above) uses silk to trap its prey. It lines a hole in the ground with silk, makes a silk trap door to cover the entrance, and lays threads as "trip wires" from the entrance to nearby twigs. It goes to the bottom of the hole and makes a false bottom to hide under. Then it waits to pounce on its prey.

Spiders hunt in different ways, many use silk. Beautiful webs like the orb web pictured right are probably the ones most of us see.

Making a web uses a lot of energy, so spiders repair them if they are damaged. They also clear away any bits of leaf or grass that have blown onto them, so insects will not spot the web.

When an insect flies into the web the spider feels the web vibrate. As the insect struggles it becomes tangled. The spider injects its prey with poison and wraps it in silk to stop it from escaping.

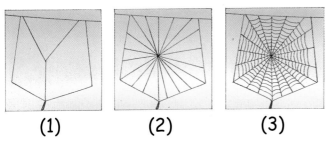

(1)   (2)   (3)

Orb spiders make webs to catch their prey (above and right). They start with a line of silk across the top, before dropping lines down at each end to make the frame, anchoring the threads to a twig or grass stem (1). Then they add the "spokes" of the web (2). Finally they add the threads that link up the spokes (3).

How Do Spiders Catch Prey?

Not all spiders catch their prey in webs or traps. Wolf spiders stalk their prey before pouncing on it. Jumping spiders, as their name suggests, catch their prey by jumping on it. The water spider does make a web, but an underwater one.

Some spiders use **camouflage**. The yellow crab spider hides in the center of yellow flowers, attacking the insects that come to sip nectar. There is even a spider that traps its prey by spitting sticky gum over it.

Spiders spin silk from the spinnerets located at the end of their abdomen. Each spinneret produces very fine threads of silk. Each strand of a spider's web is made up of many threads of silk.

Spinnerets

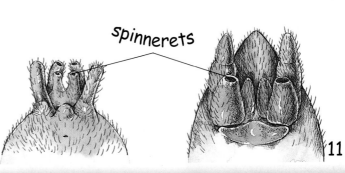

11

This orb web spider has injected its prey with poison and is wrapping it in silk (right). Soon the poison will turn the soft parts of the prey's body into liquid for the spider to suck up.

What Do Spiders Eat?

Spiders that make webs catch flying insects such as moths and flies. Others, such as trap-door spiders and wolf spiders, do not make webs. They catch insects that live on the ground. As well as insects, jumping spiders will eat the young of other jumping spiders. The large, hairy, bird-eating spiders and tarantulas of South America eat small birds, frogs, lizards, and insects.

Did You Know?

Bird-eating spiders live in the rainforests of Southeast Asia and South America. They are good at climbing trees. These spiders hunt at night so they can catch birds while they are asleep.

Spiders have claws at the end of each leg. These claws help them grip the surface of whatever they are walking on.

close up of spider's claws

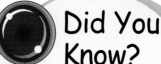

Are Spiders Good Parents?

Female spiders lay hundreds of eggs, which they protect by wrapping in a ball of silk. Many spiders then leave the ball in a safe place, such as the underside of a leaf. They do nothing more for their young.

When the eggs hatch, the spiderlings, or baby spiders, look like miniature adults. Like insects, spiders do not have a skeleton. Instead they have a hard outer case called an **exoskeleton**. To increase in size they have to molt, or shed, this case regularly and grow a new, larger one.

The lifecycle of a spider

Female wolf spider

The female wolf spider carries the ball of silk containing her eggs around with her (left).

eggs and young being carried

Some spider mothers carry their eggs on their abdomen (above). When the eggs hatch, the babies ride on her back. One European spider gives her young liquid food for a few days. Then they help her catch prey. When she dies they eat her!

How Do Spiders See?

Most spiders have eight eyes. Spiders have simple eyes – each eye has a single lens. Even though most spiders have eight eyes they cannot see very well. Instead they rely on their excellent sense of touch. The eyes of different spiders are arranged differently.

Did You Know?

At the front of a spider's head are two chelicerae. These are like a pair of pincers. Spiders use the chelicerae to hold their prey while the poison they have injected into it takes effect.

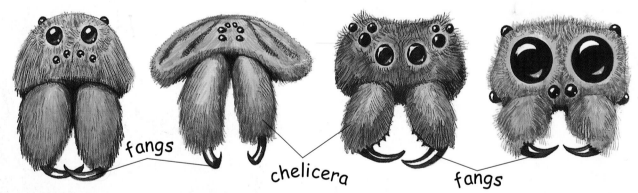

fangs

chelicera

fangs

Wolf spider   Tarantula   Jumping spider   Ogre-faced spider

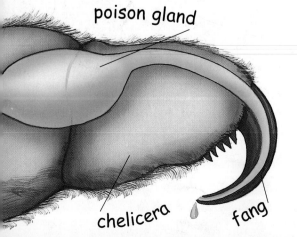

poison gland

chelicera   fang

Spiders have two fangs, one on each side of their mouth. When a spider catches prey, it bites it with its fangs. Poisonous digestive juices run from the poison gland down the hollow fangs and into the prey.

Wolf spider, showing its eyes, red chelicerae, and fangs

Spiders may have lots of eyes, but they can see little more than light and dark. By human standards that is poor eyesight. Spiders are an extremely successful group of animals that live all over world, so their eyesight must be good enough for them to survive.

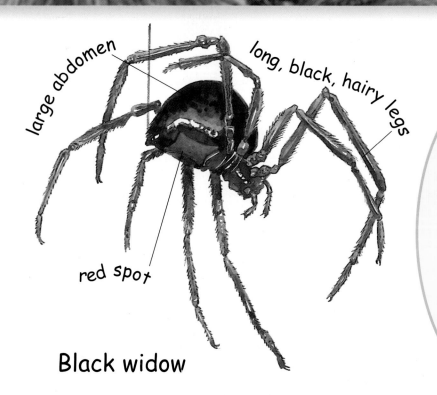

large abdomen

long, black, hairy legs

red spot

Black widow

The body of the female black widow spider measures about 1/2 inch (15 mm) across. The male measures only about 1/4 inch (5 mm).

Did You Know?

The female black widow spider makes a strong web in which to catch prey. Male black widows eat nothing. In fact, each male becomes food for a female after they have mated.

How Did the Black Widow Get Its Name?

The black widow spider lives from southern Canada to the tip of South America. Some people say it got its name because the female spider eats the male after mating, becoming a widow. Others say it got its name because its bite is so dangerous.

Ten out of every hundred people bitten by black widows in tropical areas die. The black widow is dangerous because it lives in people's homes, often hiding among clothes in cupboards.

A Brazilian banana spider

This fearsome looking spider (above) lives on the floor of rainforests in southeast Brazil. The scientific name for it is *Phoneutria keyserlingii*, named after Dr. Keyserling, the man who found it. Its bite can kill humans.

Sometimes tropical spiders reach other countries in **imported** fruit and vegetables, especially bananas. These spiders rarely live long because the climate is too cold and there is no food for them.

 Did You Know?

The tropical golden web spider lives in South and Central America. Its web, which can be over three feet (1m) wide, is so strong that local people use it to catch small fish.

Why Are Locusts Scary?

Locusts are large flying insects, like grasshoppers. Locusts eat plants and do little harm most of the time. However, female locusts lay up to 100 eggs, 12 times a year, so at times there is an enormous number of the insect that need food. They are good fliers and a swarm of locusts can fly 31 miles (50 km) a day, making the sky look dark wherever they go (see next page).

Africa

The colored areas show how a locust swarm has spread across Africa

It is difficult to know how many locusts make up a swarm, but there can be 250 million in a square mile. Some swarms in Africa have covered 1,900 square miles (5,000 sq. km) and eaten 20,000 tons of plants each day.

Locust swarm in Africa

Locust swarms are the worst in parts of Africa. They also occur in southern parts of the United States. Early settlers often found that locusts had eaten all of their crops, especially tobacco. The swarms built up without warning and then ate every green plant and tree.

Locusts are no longer a huge threat. Satellites are used to find the swarms and then aircraft spray the locusts with insecticide.

 Did You Know?

After they hatch, young locusts shed their skin six times before they become adults and can fly. Like grasshoppers, locusts have strong leg muscles. They use them to leap into the air, then they open their wings and start to fly.

Which Beetle Is the Biggest?

Beetles come in all shapes and sizes. At 1/32 of an inch (0.4 mm) long, tiny feather-wing beetles are the smallest. At the other end of the scale are the goliath, elephant, and rhinoceros beetles which can grow to 6 inches (16 cm) long. The dynastes beetle (below) lives in the rainforests of Central America. The male can grow to 7 inches (17 cm), including its horn, but the female, which has no horn, is only 4 inches (9 cm) long.

There are over 300,000 species of beetles. Some live in hot deserts, others live on high, cold mountains. The sea is the only place where beetles do not live.

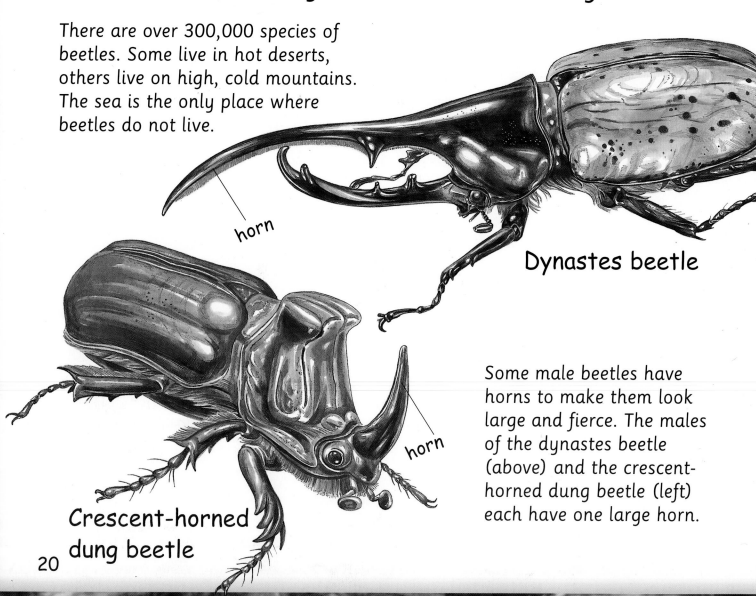

horn

Dynastes beetle

horn

Some male beetles have horns to make them look large and fierce. The males of the dynastes beetle (above) and the crescent-horned dung beetle (left) each have one large horn.

Crescent-horned dung beetle

The American cockroach (right) has infested many apartment blocks in the United States. It lives in tiny spaces under floorboards and around water pipes and enjoys the warmth of centrally-heated buildings. It gets into garbage cans and food cupboards, and can spread disease. Getting rid of cockroaches is very difficult.

American cockroach

Goliath beetle

Goliath beetles live in West African forests. They live in the treetops, eating the flowers and drinking the sap that oozes from broken twigs and branches. Goliath beetles can weigh up to 4 ounces (100 g). The female beetles, which are smaller than the males, lay their eggs in rotting tree trunks.

Why Do Wasps and Bees Sting?

Wasps and bees sting in self-defense or to protect their nest from an attacker. After it stings, wasps can always withdraw their stinger. A bee has to leave its stinger in large victims, which means the bee will die. Although it is rare for humans to die from a wasp or bee sting, some people react very badly to a sting and need medical help very quickly.

X-Ray Vision

Hold the next page up to the light and see what's inside a wasps' nest.

See what's inside

Bee collecting pollen

Bees and wasps are insects and have an exoskeleton – a tough skin on the outside of their bodies. Bees breathe through **spiracles**, which is a row of holes along each side of the body. Air goes into balloonlike **sacs** which pump the air through tubes to the rest of the body.

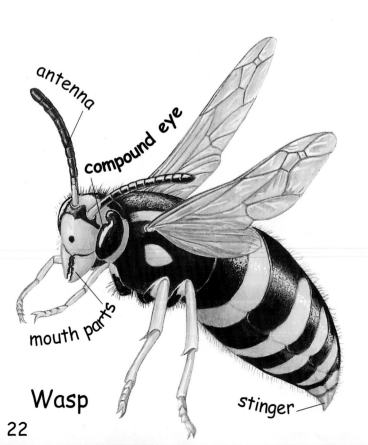

antenna

compound eye

mouth parts

Wasp

stinger

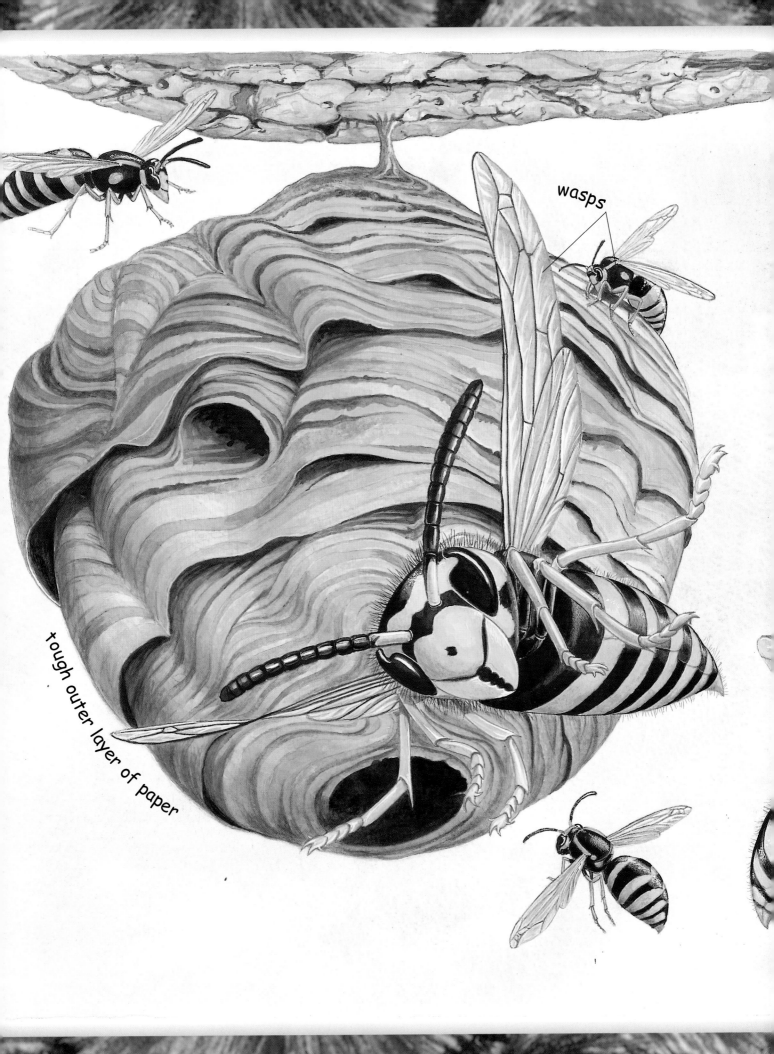

wasps

tough outer layer of paper

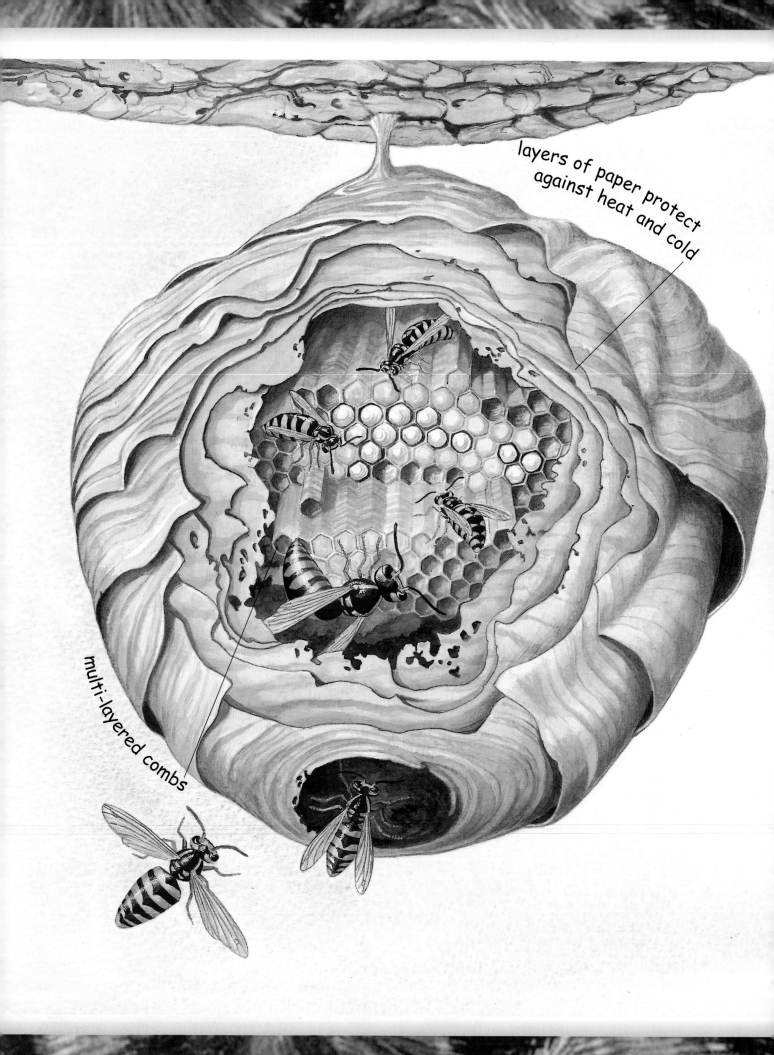

layers of paper protect against heat and cold

multi-layered combs

Do wasps chew wood?

A queen wasp chews off tiny pieces of dead wood to start her nest. When the eggs she lays in it hatch, worker wasps add to the nest in the same way. Wasps mix chewed wood with their saliva to form a paste. This paste sets into a tough "paper," from which they make their nest.

inside a wasps' nest

Yes, wasps chew dead wood to build a nest.

What's Inside a Wasps' Nest?

A wasps' nest is a busy place full of wasps coming and going. At the heart of the nest is the queen. She lays eggs. When the eggs hatch, the adult worker wasps feed the larvae with insects they catch. They also build more paper cells to make the nest larger. The larger the nest, the more eggs the queen can lay, and the more worker wasps there are to feed the larvae.

Did You Know?

Wasps catch flying insects, such as flies, by dropping on them in the air. First they bite off the fly's wings and then each of its six legs, leaving just the body. Holding the body between their legs, they carry it back to the nest to feed the larvae.

How Do Scorpions Hunt?

Most scorpions live in hot places, such as deserts. They hide under stones, in rock crevices, or in the sand during the heat of the day. Scorpions may also come into houses, crawling into clothes or shoes left on the floor.

At night, when it is cooler, scorpions hunt for spiders and insects, killing them with their pincers. Some of the big scorpions also catch geckos and small lizards. The stinger at the end of a scorpion's tail is only used in self-defense or to kill prey that struggles.

Did You Know?

Scorpions are related to spiders because they have eight legs. There are 600 different species of scorpion. They range in size from 1/2 inch (1 cm) to 7 inches (18 cm) long.

A poison gland is connected to a stinger at the end of a scorpion's tail. There are over 600 species of scorpion but only a few species are able to kill a person.

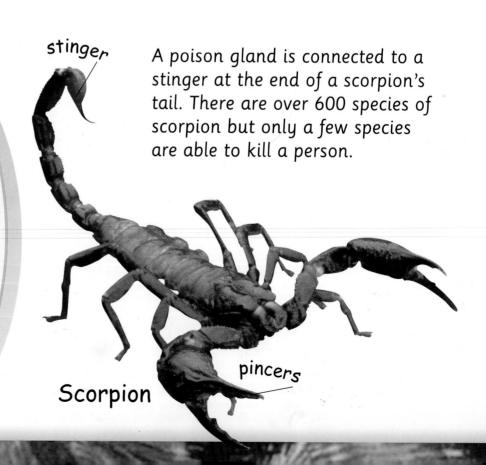

stinger

pincers

Scorpion

Did You Know?

Although they are fierce, scorpions have some **predators**. Baboons look for scorpions under stones. The baboons break off the pincers and tail so the scorpion cannot hurt them. Some lizards and snakes also eat scorpions.

Black scorpion eating a gecko

Where Do Spiders, Insects, and Minibeasts Live?

These types of creatures are very widespread. The Arctic is the only place where you won't find any spiders, insects, or minibeasts.

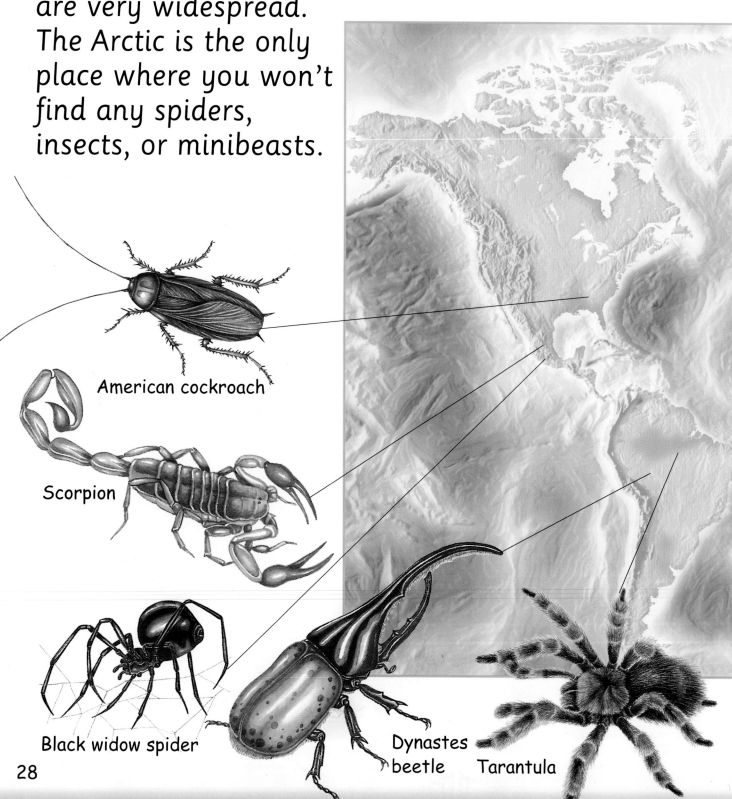

American cockroach

Scorpion

Black widow spider

Dynastes beetle

Tarantula

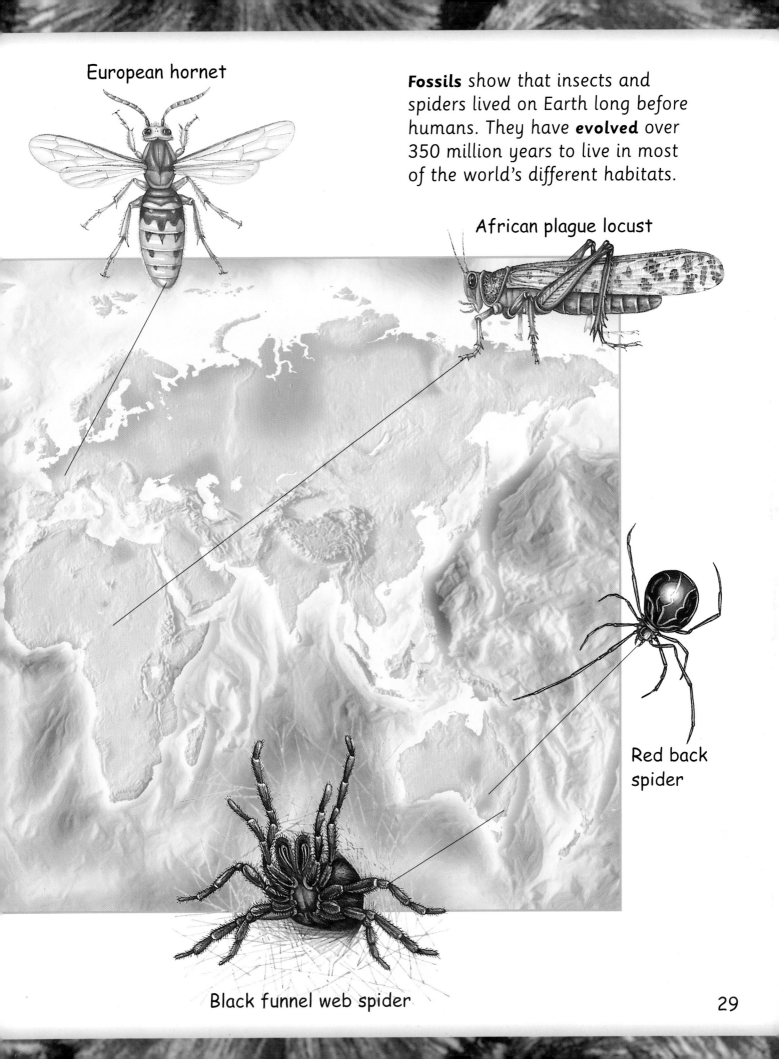

European hornet

Fossils show that insects and spiders lived on Earth long before humans. They have **evolved** over 350 million years to live in most of the world's different habitats.

African plague locust

Red back spider

Black funnel web spider

Minibeast Facts

The bolas spider doesn't spin a web to catch its prey. Instead it makes a long, strong thread with a small, sticky ball at the end. Safe on a twig, the spider dangles the thread from its front leg and swings it round and round. Any insect hit by the ball sticks to it. Then the spider pulls the thread up and kills the prey.

Arachnophobia comes from two Greek words: "arakhne" meaning spider and "phobia" meaning fear.

A scorpion has a prosoma (head and thorax together), an abdomen, and eight legs. It is neither a spider nor an insect.

Millions of years ago beetles had two pairs of wings, just as butterflies still do. Now they only have one pair because the front wings evolved into hard cases to protect the back wings.

Every day throughout the world spiders and minibeasts eat millions of insects, many of them harmful to humans.

When a male scorpion courts a female, he grabs her pincers with his own so she cannot attack him. The male must be careful after mating with the female, otherwise she might eat him.

The European water spider spends all of its life underwater. It spins a "diving bell" which it fills with air bubbles to breathe, collected at the surface of the water.

The larvae of many beetles are bigger than the adults. The body of the male goliath beetle is 4 inches (10 cm) long, but the larvae are 8 inches (20 cm) long.

There are two sorts of wasp: solitary and social. Social wasps live in groups and build big nests. Female solitary wasps build small nests. They catch spiders or caterpillars to put in the nest with their eggs. The spiders or caterpillars will become food for the larvae when they hatch.

Scorpions do not lay eggs. When the young are born, they climb onto the female's back. She carries them around with her until they are big enough to live on their own.

The hornet is a very large type of wasp. Although its bright yellow and black body makes it look scary, it only stings if it is disturbed.

The female black widow spider makes a cocoon in which she lays her eggs. Then she hangs it on a strong web and camouflages it with tiny bits of bark.

Female bird-eating spiders can live for 30 years.

Glossary

abdomen The rear, and largest, part of an insect's body.

arachnophobia An extreme fear of spiders.

camouflage Coloring or covering that makes something look like its surroundings.

cephalothorax Another word for the front part of a spider's body; also see prosoma.

cold-blooded An animal, such as a scorpion, whose body temperature varies according to the temperature of the air around it.

compound eyes The eyes of insects, made up of lots of small lenses.

evolve To develop gradually over thousands or millions of years.

exoskeleton A bony structure on the outside of a creature.

fossil The very old preserved remains of a plant or animal.

habitat A creature's natural surroundings and living place.

imported Something that has been brought from one country into another, such as food.

larva (plural **larvae**) The stage in an insect's life between hatching from an egg and becoming a pupa.

mandible Each half of an insect's jaws.

predator A creature that hunts other living creatures for food.

prey Creatures that are hunted by other creatures for food.

prosoma The front part of a spider's body.

pupa (plural **pupae**) The stage in many insects' lives between larva and adult.

sac A small pouch in which things are carried.

species A group of living things that look alike, behave in the same way, and can interbreed.

spiracle A small hole where air enters an insect's body.

thorax The middle of the three parts of an insect's body.

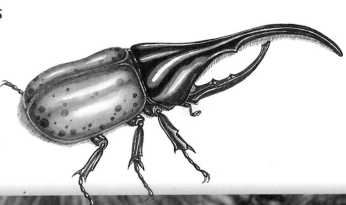

Index